The Consumer's Guide to Custom Home Building:

Simple Tips for Turning Your Dream Home into a Livable Reality

By Tim Rice, President
Whitestone Custom Homes

Copyright © 2013 by Tim Rice

All Rights Reserved

ISBN-13: 978-1490437224

ISBN-10: 1490437223

Table of Contents

Introduction: Every Home Should Be a Custom Home 7
    Fear Can be Either Debilitating--or Motivating 8
    To Build or Buy: You're Ready for a Change 9
    Debunk the Myths of Home Building, Get What You Want 11
    What You'll Find in This Book 13
    Your Dream Home Starts with a Firm Grasp of Reality 14

Chapter 1: A Recipe for Success 19
    From Builder to Boss: The Custom CEO 20
    From Dreamer to Dream Homes: The Origins of My Success 28
    Embarking on an Adventure: Don't Leave Without a Road Map 30
    Criteria for Success: You May Not Want to Build a Home If… 31
    Value Engineering: The Science of Dreams 35
    Our Concierge Service: Let Us Help You Help Yourself 37
    Moving on Up: What to Do With Your Old House 43
    The Evolution of Custom Home Building 45
    Your Recipe for Success Starts at Home 47

Chapter 2: To Build, Buy New, Buy Used, Or Don't Move? 55
    Leave Your Options Open 56
        Buy New 57
        Buy Used 58
        Stay Home 59
        New is Better; Custom New is Best! 60

Questions Lead to Answers: Prioritizing the Process _____ 60

Building for Success: It's a Family Affair _____ 66

Parting Words _____ 67

Chapter 3: The Basics of Successful Home Design _____ 69

Getting it Down on Paper: Starting with a Vision _____ 70

An Eye for Design: The Best of Both Worlds _____ 73

Needs Vs. Wants: Where the Rubber Hits the Road _____ 75

The Four Elements of Home Design _____ 77
- *Kitchen* _____ 77
- *Family Room* _____ 78
- *Master Bedroom* _____ 80
- *Master Bath* _____ 81

It's Not Just You: Designing for Resale _____ 83

Chapter 4: Advanced Home Design _____ 85

Designing for Cost _____ 87

Price as You Go: Designing by Cost _____ 88

Picture It As You Go: Crude by Design _____ 90

How Your House Gets So Expensive: Foot by Foot _____ 91
- *Square feet* _____ 91
- *Plumbing* _____ 92
- *Cabinets!* _____ 93
- *Complexity* _____ 94
- *Porches* _____ 95
- *Fancy Interior finishing* _____ 96

Parting Words: Nothing Is Ever Perfect _____ 96

Chapter 5: The Colors of Your Life _____ 99

The Designer Touch: Bringing Your Style to Life _____100

Professional Help Makes All the Difference _____103

Fear x Excitement = Transformation _____105

Be Aware of Current Trends _____107

Keeping It In House _____109

Color Choice: A Two-Part Process _____112

Parting Words: The Colors of Your Life _____115

Chapter 6: The Construction Phase _____ 117

The Process of Discovery: Your New Hobby?!? _____118

Understanding the Construction Process _____121

Step by Step Home Design: The Construction Phase _____124

Step 1: PHR # 1 _____ 124
Step 2: PHR # 2 _____ 125
Step 3: PHR # 3 _____ 130
Step 4: PHR # 4 _____ 133

Chapter 7: Mortgage, Closing Decisions & Title Companies 135

Experience Comes With Practice _____135

Fast, Good or Cheap, But Not All of the Above _____137

Making a Commitment _____138

Closing Counts _____143

Chapter 8: Moving In – And Living In – Your Home _____ 145

Conversational Facts versus Real Facts _____146

The Best Offense is a Good Defense _____149

Home Maintenance 101: Top Tips for Max Home Performance 150

Warranties 150
Photographic Evidence 151
Reminders 152

Parting Words about Moving in-And Living In-Your New Home 156

Conclusion: Home Sweet Home 159

ABOUT THE AUTHOR 163

Introduction
Every Home Should Be a Custom Home

So, you're in the market for a new home.

At least, I assume you, are if you're picking up a book called *The Consumer's Guide to Custom Home Building*. My name is Tim Rice, and as founder and CEO of Whitestone Custom Homes, I'll be your guide through the process of choosing, and even building, your new home.

And, it *is* a process. So, one of my goals in writing this book is to help you understand the process of taking the idea of a new home through all the various stages of design, style and livability. This will ultimately allow you the confidence to move forward with your dream and improve your life.

Fear Can be Either Debilitating--or Motivating

One of the reasons you've probably picked up this book is out of fear. Not "run for your life" fear, but the kind of fear that you might make a $500,000 to $1 million mistake and be forced to live with it--live *in* it--for the next 20 to 30 years.

Well, you wouldn't be alone. In my experience, the two biggest obstacles that keep new home owners/builders from "taking the plunge" are fear and misunderstanding. Why? Because, first of all, they don't know that there is a process, and even if they do, they don't quite know what that process is.

But, building a home is like anything else in life; the first step is the hardest, but a most important and crucial part of the process. If you were going to do anything else for the first time, such as planting an oak tree in your yard or building your own pizza oven, the first thing you'd do is research it, right? You might buy a book or two, Google the topic and watch a few videos, that kind of thing.

Well, buying or building a new home is no different. Don't let fear or misunderstanding keep you on the bench for another day. Allow me to walk you through the process, instead.

Fear can be a good instinct. Some people simply shouldn't build a new home but should, instead, purchase a new home from an existing inventory of homes. Which type are you? We'll decipher that in the following pages so that you are fully armed with information and caution before making a costly plunge that could end up in disappointment, if you make the wrong choice.

Is your dream home one you build from scratch or one you run across in an existing inventory of new homes? We'll find the answer together in the coming pages.

To Build or Buy: You're Ready for a Change

I love what I do because I help people's dreams come true. Everyone who comes into one of my Model

Homes at Whitestone Custom Homes is ready for something new; ready for a change. Most of them have lived in "off the rack," non-custom designed homes all their lives and are ready to build the house of their dreams from the ground up. Others loved their last home, but after the children grew up and moved out, they were ready for something new; ready for something "more their size."

It might be a bigger house, or just a "better" house. It might be sleeker, or in a better neighborhood, or have the pool they always wanted, or the mother-in-law's apartment or a three car garage.

Buying or building a home can be an emotional decision for some, and having a process--as well as knowing that process--helps take some of the emotions, including fear and misunderstanding, out of the equation. Knowing how to start, knowing what comes next, knowing what pitfalls to avoid and which paths to follow can all help you avoid mistakes, and do so with confidence.

This should be an exciting time for you and I hope this book only adds to that excitement. The fact that you have questions, and that you're beginning to look for answers, is exciting in itself.

We all love the thrill of starting something new, and there is nothing more rewarding for me than to watch a couple come into our Model Homes with that extra "pep in their step" as they prepare for the adventure of building or buying a new home.

Debunk the Myths of Home Building to Get What You Want

There are a lot of myths out there about building your first home:

- **That it will quickly become a money pit and swallow your savings whole**
- **That contractors only exist to rob you blind**
- **That it will take forever**
- **That you never end up getting what you really want…**

I'm here to debunk many of those myths so that you can make clear-headed choices and decide on your own terms how to proceed. It's true enough that some may have gone broke building a new home, but was it the contractor's fault? A misunderstanding about the process? Or both?

For instance, it's a common assumption that, to build a home from scratch, you first need to consult with an architect. But which architect? I've seen many a client bring in blueprints for "dream homes" that, quite frankly, were so unrealistic they looked more like something out of a science fiction novel.

I've heard from other clients that they'd previously tried to build a home, but after pricing the architect's specs, never pursued it because the house in question was simply too expensive to actually build.

Other clients tell horror stories of small custom home builders who quoted them one price--and one due date--only to add more and more cost and completion days onto the original bid as time marches on.

What can happen in that case is a $500,000 home, which isn't cheap to begin with but worth it if it's your "dream" home, can quickly become an $800,000 home, with no visible improvements over the original blueprints, due to hidden costs or unforeseen obstacles.

At Whitestone Custom Homes we lay it all on the line before the first shovel goes into the ground. That is a part of the process I'm talking about. The more you know, the more details you get into, the clearer your goals and the deeper you get involved in the process, the less fear you will experience and the less vulnerable you'll be to some of the myths – real or imagined – that are associated with home building.

What You'll Find in This Book

To help you understand both the process and the pitfalls of homebuilding, this book offers you the following:

- **A Recipe for Success**
- **To Build, Buy New Or Stay Home?**

- **The Basics of Successful Home Design**
- **Advanced Home Design**
- **The Colors of Your Life (i.e. the decorating process)**
- **The Construction Phase**
- **Mortgage, Closing Decisions and Title Companies**
- **Moving In--And Living In--Your Home**

Building Your Dream Home Starts with a Firm Grasp of Reality

Chances are you know exactly what you want in your dream home, from how many bedrooms to what the bathroom fixtures look like, to the fireplace mantel to where you'll put your Christmas tree; it's a vivid picture in your mind.

But it's just as likely that you've spent far less time envisioning what the actual process of building your home will look like. For instance, who is responsible for picking out those bathroom fixtures? You, the home builder, or the contractor?

How long will building the home take? Where will you live during construction? How much will that add to the final "price" of the home? Each one of these questions adds to the stress of building a home.

While you may be detail-oriented in your personal life, and the vision of your dream home may be extremely detail-oriented, the reality is that there are hundreds, if not thousands, of choices to make when building a home. Not just what type of French doors you want, but are the window panes up to code, which hinges both look best with that set of doors and are also the most durable and cost effective?

I leave as much of the creative process as possible to my clients, and try to take the stress off the rest by making choices that I know will match their dreams of visions. How many of you first think of "door stoppers" when the words "dream home" comes to mind? (You know, those little rubber tips behind your door that stops it from slamming into the wall each time you open up?) Very little, I would imagine, and yet the typical two-story, four-bedroom, two-and-a-half bath home can have several dozen door stoppers.

Whether you're a door stop aficionado or not, my point is that we make it simple for you, not more complex. The choices are always up to you, but we help as much as we can--or as little as you need. In this case, we pick the latest fashions and trends on a regular basis and put them in packages so buyers can pick items in clear groups from the latest, most popular and fashionable trends.

Do you want to stop everything and pick those out? Or would you prefer someone who knows you, is working for you--and *with* you--to achieve your vision go pick those out for you?

This is another part of the process that, knowing beforehand, can relieve some of the stress--even some of the fear--from the equation. The last thing we want is for building your dream home to turn into your home-building nightmare!

Parting Words: *Practical Luxury*

Every home should be a custom home. At least, that's my philosophy anyway, and at Whitestone Custom homes one of our trademarked catchphrases is "Practical luxury™." For me, that means that the dream home of your future will exist with the perfect balance between **cost** and **design**.

The process that you learn in *The Consumer's Guide to Custom Home Building* will help you avoid the pitfalls associated with building and buying your dream home. Armed with the process that I'll give you, the knowledge that I'll share and the experience that you'll gain by reading this book, you will spend your money in the right way and in the right place to ensure that you're achieving practical luxury.

I'll give you the tools that you need to communicate with everyone involved in the construction of your dream home; from the builder to the lender and the contractor to the laborers, to the interior decorator.

I'll help you know what to expect and when so that you can avoid being taken advantage of. You've already taken the first step to building or buying your dream home by picking up this book. The blueprint for your home building success starts on the very next page…

Chapter 1:
A Recipe for Success

Cooking an extravagant meal without a recipe is a lot like trying to build a custom home without a blueprint; you might as well do it with a blindfold on.

The best chefs know that, yes, you can adapt or even personalize a recipe to your own specific tastes once you've **mastered the process**, but until then it's best to follow directions if you want to achieve any kind of success.

In this chapter, I am going to give you the recipe for success you'll need to not only envision a home realistically, but also realistically deal with a custom home builder to find success in a collaborative and cooperative professional relationship.

First I thought it might help to hear about my own recipe for personal and professional success. In other words, why did I start WhiteStone Custom Homes?

From Builder to Boss: The Custom CEO

Long before I became the founder and CEO of my own custom home building company, I worked for many, many years building what the industry calls "production line" homes. In fact, I eventually became a Division President of a publicly held home builder.

Along the way, I worked in almost every possible job in the home building universe. I started in customer service, basically manning the complaint department and learning, every day, what ticked customers off – and how to avoid it.

Later, I built homes from the ground up, not only as a Construction Manager but, later, as a Project Manager. The experience gave me a bird's eye view of every phase of the construction process, from the nuts and bolts details of building a home to the larger picture of turning all those smaller details into a grand vision for the customer.

Eventually I became a full-fledged City Manager, where I learned how single homes fit into the larger scheme of things such as neighborhoods, subdivisions, planned communities and even cities themselves.

Finally, before I went into business for myself, I ended my employee status as a Division President for a publicly traded home builder, an experience I recommend for every home builder to learn how NOT to build homes, treat customers and plan communities!

Not every production line home builder is the same, but what I found in decades of working for such companies is that what most of them care about is the bottom line; it's not just their homes that seem to come straight off the production line, but they have a severe corporate mentality as well, in that all they care about is the bottom line profit.

Now, this is not to say that I run a charity! At Whitestone Custom Homes, we obviously care about profit, too. I believe the success of our company is proof positive that satisfied home buyers believe we do a great job. In fact, this company has had been profitable every year it has been in business. The difference between inventory, off the rack home builders and Whitestone Homes is our focus. We are not a bull in a china store outfit, bullying folks into buying from us – and only us. In other words, we don't dominate an area so that a prospective home buyer has little choice if they want something new. We happily co-exist among other companies but try to stand out in a way that is unique, personal and always, always customer based.

We *must* be customer focused to survive during an era with a shrinking market and expanding competition. Additionally, it is not money that gets us up every day and fired up about our prospects. It's building great homes. We are dedicated to building the best fit and finish in San Antonio, and it shows.

But, at the big box home builders, at the off-the-rack suppliers, it's not "How great can I make these homes?" it's "How much can I get away with, safely and legally, and still make the most profit from each home?" It's not quality these companies care about so much as quantity; more means more, after all; more homes means more people living in them and that means more money. There are hundreds of ways a builder can cut corners by hiding things behind the walls. We are not one of those builders.

I can clearly remember sitting in a meeting with the CEO of the companies I worked for. We were in the board room, myself and a dozen or so other division presidents from their territories gathered around a giant table, and we'd been given an agenda for the meeting; an itemized list of topics the CEO wanted to cover in the meeting.

One of them was customer service, which got me pretty excited because what I loved most about my job was putting real people in real homes; the personal satisfaction of making the American dream of home ownership come true for my customers.

I sat through what seemed like an endless round of talks about the financial success of the company, areas for growth, future prospects, etc., and when we finally got to the area of the agenda marked "customer service," the CEO said, and I quote, "I just assume you guys are going to improve your customer service, so we don't really need to go over that."

The meeting ended shortly after that and I sat there stunned. What stung the most, for me and some of the other division presidents there that day, was that we'd actually prepared some hard-charging initiatives to specifically and dramatically improve customer service, companywide, and this guy cared about none of that.

And he wasn't alone. Working in the industry for so long, I eventually learned that this attitude came to sum up most of the CEOs at most of the big production home builders out there; profits first, customers last.

As a business owner myself these days, I understand how important money is. After all, you can't make customers satisfied if you can't stay in business! =

It was shortly after this meeting that the idea of starting my own company came into much sharper focus. Then, too, I noticed that in the home building industry you basically had two types of builders:

1.) Production home builders like Toll Brothers, D.R. Horton, Pulte, etc.
2.) High end custom home builders like Don Craighead Homes, Burdick Custom Homes, Mike Holloway, etc.

That's it; there was nobody in between, at least, not back when I was coming up through the ranks. You either had to buy "off the rack" homes from a dozen or less floor plans or hit the lottery so you could build a custom home for millions of dollars.

If you weren't quite a millionaire but did want to build and design your own home, you had to go what we in the industry call a "pickup truck builder." In other words, a guy who would help you build your house but you'd have to finagle everything else yourself; the financing, permits- you might as well go grab a tool belt and do it yourself.

I saw a need for the folks in the middle; folks like myself who didn't want an "off the rack" house like everybody else on the street but who had neither the time, talent or inclination to work side by side with a small-time home builder to basically "do it myself."

So, I started Whitestone Custom Homes to answer that need in the marketplace. To provide a middle ground between production-built homes and a do-it-yourself kit that was wildly unrealistic for 99 percent of average home buyers.

And it all started with a recipe:

You CAN Fulfill Your Custom Home Building Dreams: *All You Need is a Recipe*

If you've ever tried to complete a home improvement project on your own, no doubt you've had a taste of what building an entire home can feel like. But that's the great distinction; with Whitestone Custom Homes, you're not doing it yourself.

You can be involved in as much or as little of the home building process as you'd like, according to your own individual recipe for success; the recipe we provide you with--be it in our offices or by reading this book. In fact, your input is mission critical to the home's final design. It won't take much effort on your part, but if we are at least pointed in the right direction, chances are we will be able to give you exactly what you want!

This recipe is useful because it breaks down the custom home building process into bite size, affordable chunks. Price is a HUGE issue for my clients. Not particularly because they can't afford to build their own homes--they can, and so can you. It's because the prospect of building a home can be so daunting, particularly when considering the "money pit" myths we talked about in the last section.

What's more, many families who assume that building their own, custom home is out of their price range and go to a production home builder instead find themselves paying much, much more than if they'd simply started by building their own homes in the first place.

The problem is with perception, and that's why we at Whitestone Custom Homes® use the tagline:

"Practical luxury™." That's because we work with you to build a home that you can both afford and consider luxurious because you were a part of its design, from conception to construction.

Depending on the customer, "practical luxury" offers one of two specific keywords. It will mean affordable to some, but opulence to others. Keep in mind that for us, a "budget" home usually begins at around $300,000 or more. So, we are not talking about peanuts, but as with everything else in life, a value home means a financial commitment. Practical luxury means that we won't waste a cent in creating your *true* dream home!

From Dreamer to Dream Homes: The Origins of My Success

As I sit down to write these words, I've been building homes for nearly 30 years (29, to be exact!). I started off in this business as a customer service rep, doing a lot of the work myself in those early days. I caulked, I painted, I put up sheet rock, and I did drywall patches and plumbing repairs, whatever the frontline customer needed to be happy.

I progressed all the way to construction superintendent, then later to construction supervisor, on up to project manager. I progressed through sales and production and witnessed the home building process, literally, from the ground up.

From wearing the tool belt myself, to handing it to someone else and watching what they did, to sitting in board rooms and focus groups and sales meetings, and everything in between. I've worked for independent and publicly held companies, some great bosses and some horrible ones. I've led work crews that I'd trust to rebuild the White House and others I wouldn't trust to tie their own shoes.

Along the way, I got my Masters in Business Administration, became a Parade of Homes judge for multiple Parades, and was the Chairman of the National Association of Home Builders Builder 20 Group. Finally, after decades working for, with, and under other home builders, and studying home building inside and out, up and down, and from side to side, I opened Whitestone Custom Homes in 1998.

You Are About to Embark on an Adventure: Don't Leave Without a Road Map

Building a home is not like buying a home. One, buying a home is a destination; building a home is a journey. In fact, it's more like an adventure. There is newness around every corner; something exciting or original or unique or jaw-dropping to discover.

Whether it be a unique floor plan, installing an Infinity pool, vaulted ceilings that inspire awe or imported deck pavers, watching a dream home evolve before your very eyes is an experience – an adventure – unlike few others in life.

From getting your plans designed to watching them come to life, every day is a journey. Imagine an empty lot, a flat blueprint, a level foundation and then, day after day, a home is built. From the concrete and the walls to the interior and the roof to the flourishes, finishing touches and bells and whistles. It's like watching a child grow up right before your very eyes.

And, just like new parents, every day of raising that child gives you the confidence for another day; and another. Every first fever, ever first cough, every first word or first step makes you more confident in your skills as a parent.

Likewise, it's fascinating for me to watch "new" home builders quickly adopt the language, the lingo and, yes, the confidence about building their own custom home as they go through the process for themselves. One day they're fawning over blueprints and the next they're correcting contractors and handing out hard hats to impressed visitors.

Criteria for Success: You May Not Want to Build a Home If…

I've said it before and I'll say it again: Building a home is NOT for everybody. What seems like an adventure to some can turn into a nightmare for others, especially if you don't particularly enjoy getting your hands dirty or being a decision-maker.

So, who *shouldn't* build their own home? Well, I strongly recommend that you *don't* build a house if:

- **You're happy with the status quo.** If you like things the way they are, if you're resistant to change or don't feel the need for change, don't build your own home. Contentedness is a powerful feeling. If you're happy where you are, why go on the home building adventure in the first place? Too often, couples get carried away by the momentum of building a home when they're actually unprepared for, and not even that fond of, the process involved. If you're happy where you are, I suggest you stay there until you're not! Building a new home is definitely an improvement in your life. For many, it is the next step to greater happiness for themselves and their family. But some people are simply too happy – or too scared – to venture out.

- **It's not a unanimous decision.** Everyone living in the house, or at least the ones paying for it, should definitely agree that you both want to build a new home before making the plunge. I've seen many cases where one spouse is merely "going along to get along" with the other, who desperately wants to build a new home. We realize there will be the most convinced spouse. That is only natural, but to be truly happy, both spouses must be convinced.
- **You like old technology.** The modern world of custom home building is not only high-tech but cutting edge and fast paced. It can get overwhelming if you're not prepared for the changes that have happened in the construction industry over the last five to ten years, or are unwilling to adopt them.
- **You are a perfectionist.** If you seek perfection in every area of your life, particularly your living space, you should probably avoid building a

custom home at all costs. Custom homes <u>are not</u> extruded out of a machine in some factory, but manufactured homes are. Those are homes that, like cars off an assembly line, come pre-assembled and popped out in cookie cutter fashion, with no muss, no fuss and, above all, no surprises – or frustration.

- **You can't expect, or appreciate, the unexpected.** Part of the reason why home building is such an adventure, just like child rearing, is that the only constant you can expect is the unexpected. Plans are just that- plans. They're written in ink, not stone, and the biggest part of the home building adventure is seeing how your dream translates into reality. The best custom home builders are realists who not only know when to compromise, but how to pick their battles. Part of the joy of the home building process is being there every step of the way, for every brick or stone that goes up, watching the house evolve. <u>While custom homes are never perfect, they are personal; it's hard not to get attached to something you watch grow from the ground up.</u> This new home will be your design. Your ideas brought to life! However, if you can't appreciate or expect the unexpected, then building a custom home probably isn't for you.

Value Engineering: The Science of Dreams

How do we help customers turn their dream home into a reality? At Whitestone Custom Homes, we start with something we call Value Engineering.

Value Engineering is our way of living up to our tag line of "Practical Luxury™." We want to provide you with the best house possible within your budget. Whatever the budget, we don't want to waste your money. We'd rather put your money to good use in ways that add value to the home, but don't add excessive costs. So we examine the plan for your home with a critical eye, playing devil's advocate with every inch of the blueprint and floor plan to ensure that there are no hidden costs, surprises, wasted money or efforts.

Something as simple as the flooring in your living room can take on great meaning when you match the kind of tiles or hardwood flooring your using with the actual size or dimensions of the room. Will you end up cutting a fourth of your tiles, or lopping off two feet of every eighth floorboard, because of the dimensions?

Building a home from scratch allows us to closely examine every foot of every room, match it to the variables in your fixtures, wall coverings, etc., and "Value Engineer" the home for maximum value and minimal cost from the front door to the attic insulation.

People come to us for very specific reasons, and oftentimes those reasons involve significant life changes that are occurring within the family unit. The reason our homes are not only custom built but custom designed is because there is no cookie cutter formula or template that works for every home buyer.

Maybe your children are leaving the home and you're looking for a smaller, sleeker, and more streamlined and open floor plan to fit your new lifestyle. Maybe you have two children in college who still come home from time to time and need room, but not as much room; or just one room. Maybe you're adding children and need more room.

Maybe you've just gotten divorced or remarried. Maybe you're newly single and are looking for that ultimate Sex & the City bachelorette pad or man cave, or maybe you've just married into a blended family ala The Brady Bunch!

Whatever the personal issues in the home, you're ready for a change and we want to take charge of the process for you; Value Engineering helps us do just that.

Our Concierge Service: Let Us Help You Help Yourself

When clients come to see us, they often know "exactly" what they want but not quite how to get it.

They may know they want a pool, but not what shape, how big or how deep. They may know they want a built-in island in the kitchen but do they want the sink there, or a mini-fridge underneath, or a marble baking top, etc.

To avoid confusion, we have a variety of forms that we have clients fill out that guides them through the process, digging for details and slowly drawing them down a "design funnel" until they have narrowed their choices down enough to make definitive, deliberate decisions.

One such form is our Concierge Form. As the name implies, this form acts as a do-it-yourself guide to your new dream home. (You can find the actual form below, PLUS on our website at http://whitestonehomes.com/.) It lists such categories as:

- **General must have items** (i.e. view of hills, warm feeling, Tuscan elevation, lots of closet space)

- **Kitchen must have items** (i.e. stainless steel appliances, gourmet serving island, two dishwashers)
- **Garage must have items** (i.e. three car, built in cabinets, epoxy floor covering, freezer plug, air-conditioned, surround sound)
- **Etc.**

Through every room in the house, plus the front, side and back exterior, every bathroom, closet and cabinets, we walk you through it, step-by-step. We get you familiar with industry specific terms, like "judges paneling," "Tuscany elevation" and "full arbor."

For every room or category there are five lines to help list the major needs from the minor, drilling down deeper and deeper on every choice, until it's clear to you what exactly you want, what you can live without, and what compromises may need to be made to reach a livable budget.

It may sound clinical, but as you go through the process, complete with visuals and even 3-D modeling, if needed, you can feel the excitement build for each new client. This is where dreams become a reality, where the sometimes hard choices are made, but where the picture becomes real and solid in their heads.

By the time we're through filing this in, everyone knows what to expect; you, me, the builder, the designer, the sub-contractors, we're all on the same page together.

WhiteStone Custom Homes, Ltd.®
CONCIERGE
Design/Build Service

BUYERS NAME: _____
ADDRESS: _____
BASE PLAN NAME: _____
PRICE W/ LOT PREMIUM: _____

COMMUNITY: _____
LOT: _____ BLOCK: _____
TARGET PRICE ALL IN: _____

CIRCLE ONE: Her List   His List   Combined List
              Kid #1   Kid #2   Kid #3

GENERAL MUST HAVE ITEMS (i.e. view of hills, warm feeling, Tuscany elevation, lots of closet space)
1. _____
2. _____
3. _____
4. _____
5. _____
6. _____

KITCHEN MUST HAVE ITEMS (i.e. stainless steel appliances, gourmet serving island, two dishwashers)
1. _____
2. _____
3. _____
4. _____
5. _____
6. _____

MASTER BEDROOM MUST HAVE ITEMS (i.e. minimum 18' wide, fireplace, 12' ceilings, and view)
1. _____
2. _____
3. _____
4. _____
5. _____
6. _____

MASTER BATH MUST HAVE ITEMS (i.e. two shower heads, 6' whirlpool tub, granite tops, frameless glass)
1. _____
2. _____
3. _____
4. _____
5. _____
6. _____

ENTRY WAY MUST HAVE ITEMS (i.e. open to living area, two story entry, and wood floors)
1. _____
2. _____
3. _____
4. _____
5. _____

STUDY MUST HAVE ITEMS (i.e. judges paneling, wood floors, build in desk & bookshelves)
1. _____
2. _____
3. _____
4. _____
5. _____
6. _____

BEDROOM # 2	BEDROOM # 3	BEDROOM # 4	BEDROOM # 5
1. _____	1. _____	1. _____	1. _____
2. _____	2. _____	2. _____	2. _____
3. _____	3. _____	3. _____	3. _____
4. _____	4. _____	4. _____	4. _____
5. _____	5. _____	5. _____	5. _____

EXTERIOR FRONT MUST HAVE ITEMS (i.e. stucco w/ banding, stucco w/ stone, Tuscany look, brick detail w/ stone)
1. _____
2. _____
3. _____
4. _____
5. _____

EXTERIOR OUT DOOR LIVING MUST HAVE ITEMS (i.e. 20' x 14' cedar deck, outdoor kitchen w/ tv, full arbor, 10' x 14' covered patio)
1. _____
2. _____
3. _____
4. _____
5. _____

GARAGE MUST HAVE ITEMS (i.e. 3 car, built in cabinets, epoxy floor covering, freezer plug, air-conditioned, surround sound)
1. _____
2. _____
3. _____
4. _____
5. _____

MISCELLANEOUS MUST HAVE ITEMS (i.e. basketball hoop @ driveway)
1. _____
2. _____
3. _____
4. _____
5. _____

Figure 1.1: *The Whitestone Custom Homes Concierge Form*

Moving on Up: What to Do With Your Old House

Many of our clients naturally come to us while living in current homes and needing to sell them by the time their new home is ready. We've all heard horror stories of folks selling a home too soon before their new home is ready, and forced to live in the Motel 6 down the road from the construction site for a few months until it's finished. Likewise, we've all heard of those families who wait too long to sell and end up paying two mortgages until they can unload their first home.

While it is impossible to time the build to your exact move date, we can make the whole process less stressful by improving the odds of your old home selling and you easily moving into your new home. Our sales counselors have the details of this program and can help you eliminate most of the stresses of "switching houses."

Our "Move Up" program helps you sell your own home by partnering you with one of our team of qualified real estate agents who understand the needs of the new home buyer, as opposed to just being a realtor who's trying to sell your home. (This is someone that we use only if you are not currently working with a Real Estate Broker. If you are, great, we would be happy to work with your Realtor to build you the home of your dreams).

As of this writing, our Realtor move-up team has sold 100% of our clients' homes. What's great about this program is that the Realtors are in the loop from blueprint to building permits to rock or brick laying, so they know when you need to move into your new house, how long you'll need to stay in the old one, and pretty much everything in between.

This program becomes increasingly important as many clients need to actively sell their old home in order to be able to afford a new one, and our realtor partners can help facilitate that process before, during and after construction of your new home.

The Evolution of Custom Home Building

Home building as we know it, be it assembly line, cookie cutter production homes or custom homes, is still relevantly in its infancy. Once upon a time, people that wanted to build a new home were pretty much on their own. You had to go find your own roofers, electricians, tile guys, plumbers, brick layers and everyone in between.

Anyone who wanted to build a new home was basically the master of their own domain; securing the financing, buying the plot and then corralling each and every contractor under their own steam.

Companies like Sears were the early forerunners of later home builders like Ryland Homes, Toll Brothers and Pulte in that they could ship prefabricated homes to your lot and even help set them up for you, but it wasn't until all those GI's began returning home from World War II, needing homes for their young families, that the true construction boom and the subsequent rise of manufactured home builders began in the United States.

The Levitt Brothers out of New York were masters at meeting their customer's needs and providing manufactured homes at reasonable prices. Their work in the early history of "planned communities" – i.e. vast suburban plots of cookie cutter "tract homes" – is immortalized today in Levittown, New York, an entire city, or "planned community," of manufactured homes.

Planned communities and the suburban enclaves they created became the "new norm" for American homeowners tired of being crammed together in high-rise city apartment buildings.

But that only helped if you wanted an "off the rack" house, something just like everybody else's on the block where you might go into the sales office, pick from House A, B or C, pick your flooring, wall covering and grout color and away you go.

True custom home builders – who would do the work of corralling contractors, designing blueprints, pulling permits, even getting financing, etc. – still only existed for the wealthy until the last few decades.

Today, of course, massive conglomerate home builders like Toll Brothers and Pulte are publicly traded companies who don't just build one community at a time, but multiple communities all over the country.

Your Recipe for Success Starts at Home

In preparation of your new dream home, it's important to plan early. Like newly engaged couples devouring every bridal magazine and book on the shelves, or newly pregnant mothers scouring the internet for what to expect when they're expecting, it's time to get excited about the process but also back up that excitement with research.

Here is a simple "Recipe for Success" you can start creating right now, today, as you go about turning your dream home into a reality:

1.) **Make a list; your form or our form.** Use our Concierge Form, located above, or at http://whitestonehomes.com/, to begin to "drill down" on exactly what you'd like to see in your dream home. Or make a list of your own.

2.) **Collect pictures.** I always suggest clients begin gathering together a "scrapbook" of what they'd like their dream home to look like. Start scouring through home design magazines either online, at the bookstore or in the library to get an idea of the kids or features you'd like to see in your own home. Just like bringing a picture of your favorite haircut into your hairdresser, the more detail you can provide a home builder the closer they can get to realizing your dream and making it a reality. Online options include a great site called www.Houzz.com, which bills itself as "The largest collection of interior design and decorating ideas on the Internet, including kitchens and bathrooms." A simple trip to Barnes & Noble helps. There must be a dozen or more magazines that cater to this kind of endeavor. Look at the magazines that show the style you are looking for. Is it Texas Hill Country Contemporary or Hearth and Home or Modern Tudor or Country Escape? Bring them in, dog-eared and highlighted and torn out or folded over. Together, we can help you sort through the options and show you the ones that fit your budget. Keep in mind that we will price your home based on the details in the change orders, rather than pricing exactly what is in the picture. Most of the time we do not know exactly what you want included from a picture in your new home. Additionally, we might have to make adjustments based on regional availability.

3.) **Start comparison shopping the prices in your neighborhood.** Start delving into local real estate to see what you can expect to pay for comparable houses in your dream, or ideal, neighborhood. This will help you understand current pricing and guide you on what you can expect get for the price you pay.

4.) **Collect floor plans.** Many of our clients start visiting model homes to get a feel for what's hot, and what's not, in the latest home designs. There they can collect floor plans that they like and bring them back to us as a starting point.

5.) **Print them out.** Nowadays, you can also take "virtual tours" of model homes, which allow you to print out attractive floor plans you can then bring to us. While we cannot copy plans exactly, they can be a great inspiration for your new, custom home plans. In fact, we may have the plan you need in our inventory of plans. We typically put up only so many plans on our website. We have others in archive that might work, too.

6.) **Measure the rooms.** If you're visiting a model home and particularly like the size or feel of a room, bring a tape measure and record the dimensions so we can examine how they might look in your personalized home. Oftentimes, we can achieve the feeling of "largeness," or even "intimacy," with different dimensions but skill in bringing the finished product to market. In other words, creating a 1200-square foot sunken living room might be beyond your budget, but if we know what you're looking for we can perhaps create something that looks, and even feels, the same through Value Engineering a smaller, but equally spacious-feeling room.

7.) **Get an estimate.** Oftentimes, the estimate on your dream home may be exorbitant or even prohibitive. That's why it's called an estimate; it's not written in stone. But if you've done your homework and come prepared, and are open to suggestions and honest about your must-haves and can-live-withouts, we can begin to reach a price that will also achieve your dreams.

8.) **Get clear.** One thing that's required for a successful building project is clarity. You can't be wishy-washy about what you want, or unprepared for surprises. You can't want one thing and your spouse wants another; you have to prepare a unified front. That's why this "recipe" is so critical for success; the more you steep yourself in the process, from day one, the more clarity you'll have around that process and how to make it work to your advantage.

9.) **Be prepared to compromise.** Finally, one of the most important "ingredients" to making this recipe work is your willingness to compromise on issues both big and small. The realities of time, budget, technology, available materials and a variety of other variables make compromise not just a luxury, but a necessity if you really *do* want to build your dream house in the real world!

If you do take action, you will embark on a life changing adventure with confidence. If you don't take action, you will not have confidence you can do it.

Chapter 2:
To Build, Buy New, Buy Used, Or Don't Move?

Not everyone is meant to build their own home. I frequently see clients walk into our showroom and, within minutes, I can tell they're not really good candidates for future home builders.

Maybe they've heard about how "great" home building can be from a friend or family member, or maybe their neighbor just built a home and they were impressed with how it looked. Whatever the reason, it's easy to get excited about building a custom design home, but the reality is often very different from the "dream."

Many people want to build a home for emotional reasons; and that's fine. We've already talked about how exciting it is to build your own home, to see your dream come to reality. But, a lot of folks can't see past the dream, that illusion they have of what it means to build a home, and I can tell as soon as I start talking to them that they're just not ready for the financial, emotional and physical commitment required to turn a dream into a dream home.

Leave Your Options Open

The question you have to ask yourself is, "Can I commit?" Not everyone can. Again, why would a custom home builder dissuade you from building a custom home? I'm not! But, I want to work with people who are ready, willing and able to make that commitment to the process of building a home, not just the emotion that makes them say, we should build something.

Building a custom home is not the only game in town. Never was and never will be. You have options; several of them. The way I see it, in fact, you have four choices when it comes to your home:

- **Build:** You can build a new home from scratch, which is what we'll be talking about in this book.
- **Buy New:** You can buy a new home that no one has ever lived in before.
- **Buy Used:** You can buy a home someone has lived, either directly from them or a Realtor.
- **Don't Move:** Finally, you can stay put.

Naturally, some of these options are more glamorous than others. Let's revisit a few:

Buy New

Buying a new home has a lot of great benefits, including that wonderful "all new" factor that means you won't have to turn right around and rip out the carpet or replace the air conditioner or fumigate the kids' rooms. On the other hand, it's "new," not "custom new," so you still have to abide by what the original designers built "for" you, not exactly "with" you.

Buy Used

Then, there's buying a used home, one that could be five, ten, or fifty years old. Some people love to buy used homes, fix them up, work on them during all of their spare time and make the home an ongoing project. It's a project for them, much the same way building a custom home is a project for my clients.

Others see buying a used home as a way to still get out of their rut, move into a new neighborhood, or maybe even get "more home for their money," without the added expense of a custom or new home.

Oftentimes, buying a used home is the cheapest of these four alternatives, save from staying home. Materials, technology, property, workmanship, even craftsmanship was always cheaper once upon a time in the past than it is today, and so getting a great deal on an existing, "used" home can often satisfy those emotional cravings that make folks want to build a custom home.

Of course, used homes are not new and never will be again. It's a lot like buying a used car. You could be buying a great deal…or a lemon. You simply just don't know. You can take care to assure yourself that you're getting a quality, "as is" home that won't fall down around you the minute the former owners drive away, but a lot of people still aren't comfortable with taking that risk. That's why so many people buy new homes. They want warranties, new appliances, the latest energy technology, design- the works.

Stay Home

And lastly, I know it may not sound very "sexy" to simply "stay home," but the fact is…timing is everything. If you're not ready to build a new home, either for the expense, the compromise, the time, the energy or the collaboration, staying put could save you hundreds of thousands of dollars and months'-worth of headaches.

Making decisions like these – to build a home, buy new, buy used or stay home – will never actually be easy, but there is freedom in choosing. Once you go through the process of deciding which path to home ownership is the right one for you, you can settle in, be content and do the work that needs to be done to make that goal a reality.

But first, you have to decide.

New is Better; Custom New is Best!

Let's talk straight: New homes, in my opinion, are better than older used homes simply because the advances in technology, materials, skilled labor, etc. You can start fresh.

Questions Lead to Answers: Prioritizing the Process

At WhiteStone Custom Homes, we run a showroom, not a sales floor. And, I think that's a pretty important distinction. By that, I mean we don't expect you to walk in, buy something, and leave on your very first trip. In fact, we don't want you to! Yes, we have salespeople and we want your business, but not at the cost of your peace of mind, or ours, for that matter.

I've spent so much time talking about the mentality of building a custom home because I believe it's critically important to have the right mindset before you start; even before you *decide* to start.

Here are five questions to ask yourself before deciding to build a new home:

1.) Do you have to be in control in all situations?

It takes a village to build a new custom home, and while you are most certainly the customer and eventual homeowner, you're not necessarily the "boss," if you know what I mean. The team we assemble at WhiteStone Custom Homes includes knowledgeable experts, not just in the actual construction but the planning, organizing, implementation, design and facilitating aspects of such a significant project.

You will have people making suggestions on everything from flooring and landscaping to roofing and kitchen cabinets to faucets and all the way down to the nuts, the bolts and the pitch of the roof.

All of these people will be working for you, but they will all be working under their own steam and in conjunction with one other, meaning you won't necessarily be in control of all situations at all times. Not everybody is okay with that, particularly when they're spending new custom home dollars.

2.) Are you excited by change or something new?

I always say that building a home is first an emotional decision, then a physical operation. That's because the desire to build a new home doesn't necessarily come from the smell of fresh lumber or the desire to put on a hard hat, but the stirrings of change within a particular individual, couple or family.

Building a new custom home is exciting and it *should* be exciting. You should be excited about it. It's also about change- a lot of change. You may be going from 1,500-square feet to 4,000-square feet, from single story to two-story, from apartment or townhouse to a freestanding dwelling. These changes are adjustments and require a particular level of energy to commit to.

3.) Do you need a new home?

Let's shift from the emotional to the physical and ask, "Do you straight up need a new home?" This may seem like a simple question but the fact is many people who think they "need" a new home just want one. They want what their neighbors have, what their friends or other family members have, they want to keep up with the Joneses, or simply be the Joneses. That's more want than need, and can lead to trouble when the design team start drilling down to details.

However, if the emotional want is matched with a physical need, then the motivation for building a new home becomes clearer and the process simpler. If you need a bigger house, a newer house, a smaller house, a different style of house, one with features you've always wanted and now can afford, such as a view of the setting sun, a better neighborhood for your family, a pool or garden or backyard barbecue outdoor living area, or lush landscaping, then the decision to build a custom new home simply makes more sense.

4.) Are you a perfectionist? Do people actually *call* you a perfectionist?

No home is perfect; there is always compromise. If you are a perfectionist who can't understand, abide or compromise, then the build is going to be long, arduous, unpleasant and, ultimately, unsatisfactory. Not because everyone didn't try to please you, but because perfectionists simply can't be pleased.

5.) Do you and your spouse agree/argue most of the time? (FYI, most of the time is 80 percent.)

In the next section, I talk about your "building family," but here I want to talk about your actual family, particularly your spouse. Do you argue most of the time? (And for the record, most of the time is 80 percent or more). If so, building a new home is probably not for you.

If you're fighting under ideal conditions, before you start to design and construct a new home, then imagine what it might be like when the imported Italian Tile shipment is delayed by a few days, which sets back the schedule a week, which impacts the roofing team, and the tile crew, creating a ripple effect that ultimately creates stress, challenge and delays for all involved.

Building a new home can be challenging for all couples, even the healthiest, friendliest and easiest going. But for those who already argue a significant portion of the time pre-construction, the challenges can turn the construction itself into a nightmare, which bleeds into your enjoyment of living in the home once it's actually built. Are you prepared for that? Is your spouse?

Or, think of it this way; if there is a screaming match every time you and your spouse and your family go out to eat, how much more intense are those battles going to be every time a decision needs to be made on a new home?

I ask these questions of every client, whether formally or informally. Look, we're a small family business with an A+ rating with the Better Business Bureau. That's because we really do treat your family like our family, to the point where we, a). Want to see your dream of constructing a new home become a reality but, also, b). Don't want to sell you on something you don't really want, need or are ready for.

Building for Success: It's a Family Affair

Think of building a home like taking a long trip with your extended family. Not just your wife and grown kids, but their spouses, in-laws, stepchildren, etc. Now add your travel agent!

Building a home takes time; from planning to conception to construction to completion, it's a months-long effort full of ups, downs and compromises. What you want is a team, a "building family," as we like to call it, that you'd actually like to go on vacation with for an extended time.

All parties need to go along to get along, to understand each other, to enjoy spending time with each other and, ultimately, to make important compromises based on price, technology, tools, skill, resources, etc.

I'm not saying we have to be best friends, but there should be a certain level of respect, understanding, and yes, companionship if we're going to build a house together.

Parting Words

Listen, not every home builder is going to run you through a questionnaire to see if you're up for the challenge of building a custom home with them. Most likely they assume you're grown, sane adults who can handle the stress of building a custom home and, if not, you'll either sink or swim along the way.

But, we build showcase custom homes and that requires a higher level of commitment from you and equally from us. We also consider you a part of the Whitestone family, and like all good family, we want to make sure you know what you're getting into before you start the process, not midway through!

This is a book I want to be able to hand to my family; my brother or sister, parents or uncles, nieces or nephews. So, I'm speaking to you as I would speak to them. If I could tell them what I've learned after doing this for over thirty years, this is what I would say. I wouldn't let my family rush into building a custom-designed home, so I'm not about to let you – my building family – rush into it, either.

Chapter 3:
The Basics of Successful Home Design

Designing your new home is a little like predicting the future. Oftentimes, couples come in, or families, and as we start the design process and mapping out a floor plan, I start to see cracks in the armor. The husband wants this, the wife wants that, one kid wants this and another wants that.

What it boils down to is that a lot of people don't know what they want, period. It's a little like being a kid in a candy store; there are so many options nowadays, not just in bedrooms and kitchens, but in accents, accessories, bells, whistles, landscaping and layout, that folks just start grabbing what looks good without a feel for how it all might fit together. That's a great recipe for designing a home today that you may hate a year from now!

Our job then, is to help them understand not just the aesthetics of their various single design choices, but how they all fit together. And that's the basics of successful home design.

Getting it Down on Paper: Starting with a Vision

The process of your home design begins quite simply, but realistically; in black and white. Using the Concierge Form we discussed in earlier chapters, we begin to make your dreams real by asking you to explain them. This is a breakthrough process for many clients who may know what they think they want, but only really drill down to specifics when they're forced to.

Remember, building a home is a family affair. We encourage you to include the whole family, including everyone who will be living in the home, to help design it. This can take the form of you and your spouse filling out the concierge form before discussing it with your kids, asking your kids to help you fill it out or, in certain cases, handing every family member a concierge form, or at least a blank sheet of paper, and letting them know exactly what's involved in the process.

This is a real opportunity for each family member to get down in writing what they want. This way, everybody should be happy, and more importantly, they'll know upfront what the home will look like. This way nobody can complain – spouse, child or mother-in-law – nor will be able to complain once the house is complete!

This will help everyone in the family make their voice heard when it comes to what they want…

- **In the living room;**
- **In their bedroom;**
- **In the garage;**
- **In the front yard;**
- **In the back yard;**
- **In the loft/Game room;**
- **In the outdoor cooking/living area;**

- **In the pool area;**
- **Etc.**

What's interesting about this process is that it often makes the planned home real for my clients. I can see them getting excited about fixtures and faucets and features and as they begin to envision what their new home might look like, it's almost like they get a new spring in their step.

My clients are motivated to build anyway, but this really brings it all together in a way that is both purposeful and visual. They can see the dream becoming a reality, and few feelings compare.

This process makes way for a clear and well-defined path for them to follow. Now, rather than just seeing a head full of unrelated pictures or picturing a meandering, curving mass of confusion, the line is straight and clear.

It's time consuming to consider every room, all the variables and whittle down your choices. Brick or slate?

Tuscan design or southwestern ranch style? Loft or Full Bonus Room? Hilly or flat? Game room or three car garage? These choices do take thought, time and even discussion, but as I like to say, clients evolve into "partners" in the home design and the process does require this kind of investment to pay off.

An Eye for Design: The Best of Both Worlds

Our sales staff is architecturally trained to be able to help our clients' dreams become a reality. I like to call them "translators," in addition to their other technical skills, because I often hear them listening to a client's rambling explanation of some floor plan or feature or accessory they've seen in a neighbor's house, or from the road, or in a magazine and magically our designers will not only be able to show it to them, but either draw it up on the computer or show them a sample of what it might look like in their home.

That's why the concierge form and several of the other requirements we ask for – magazine clippings, sample floor designs, web links and other visual cues – are so important. The more information you bring to us to express your vision, the closer our designers can get to making that vision a reality.

Having designed dozens of homes in a variety of styles, we have a vast catalog of existing floor plans, designs and features that we can adapt to the client's specific needs. So, building on the concierge form, our designers can blend the existing with new. This gives clients an even clearer vision when they can begin to see the house take shape, not just on paper but in living color, on screen, in print or in 3-D models – or even existing homes.

There is nothing like seeing a really great home, floor plan or design and enlisting a team of professionals to help you customize and personalize it for your individual needs.

A little bit of this house, a smidge of that floor plan, a garage here, a loft there, the landscaping this way, the lighting that way, and accent by accent, room by room, your house becomes a custom home.

Needs Vs. Wants: Where the Rubber Hits the Road

The next part of the process delves into separating what you want from what you need. We're Americans; we all want everything. More toppings, more cheese, double-size it and add sprinkles, if you please.

But when you keep in mind that each element of your home design not only affects how the house fits together but also costs more, we get down to the nitty-gritty: What do you want and what can you really afford?

Here is where the design process gets real for a lot of people, because we still want to create a dream home for them, but we want to do it within the limits of their personal, professional and financial reality.

Yes, a built-in outdoor kitchen with stainless steel fixtures, mini-bar and dorm fridge. Resort style pool and camouflaged rock speakers is what every red-blooded American homeowner wants, but do they need it? Will it fit with the rest of the house design? Will the added cost of that luxury affect the size of, say, the garage or the den or the guest room or even the pool? Will it mean the difference between an outdoor kitchen and a pool?

Here is where involving your family, and the design team, as well as compromise and lively discussion can help. We don't rush this process, but we do keep it moving for your benefit. We recognize that both the wants and needs are real to the client, so we generally take a week or two to really fill out these forms, gather these pictures, troubleshoot these issues, present the pros and cons of each feature until the client can see the forest for the trees and make clear, rational, realistic decisions.

Now we're really cooking!

The Four Elements of Home Design

Regardless of how big or small the house may be or how many rooms or square feet, Tuscan style or Santa Fe, there are really only four main elements of home design:

1.) Kitchen
2.) Family Room
3.) Master Bedroom
4.) Master Bath

Here is where I'd like to walk you through each element:

Kitchen

After thirty years in the construction industry, there is one thing I know for certain: people LOVE their kitchens. Our job is to create a kitchen that clients not only love, but will love for all the right reasons. And that leads us to some specific questions you might not think to ask, such as:

- **Where do you want the kitchen?**

- **In the middle of the house, in the front, in the back?**
- **Or, let's get more specific: Do you want it on the left leisure side of the home?**
- **The right leisure side of the home?**
- **And what do you want in it?**
- **How big will it have to be to accommodate, say, a central island or double door refrigerator or breakfast nook?**

All of these answers are critical as we move onto the next major element of home design, the family room.

Family Room

Homes are like puzzles; they must fit together, so depending on what your wants, needs and plans are for the kitchen – which is why we start with that area of the house – we can then move on to designing the family room.

If you want your kitchen on the right leisure side of the house, perhaps you'll want the family room on the left. Or vice versa! Or, maybe your kitchen is the centerpiece of your house and you really want it to blend into the family room in a way that is unique and different.

As the floor plan begins to evolve and take shape, you can see the importance of these four elements of design and how they not only fit together, but begin to inform and color the feel, tone and tempo of the home itself.

The kitchen and family room elements are also integral to the style of home you're looking for. We see a lot of Tuscan and Texas Hill Country Traditional here, as well as a kind of loft-like, farmhouse style, the castle look and the Mediterranean look, etc.

You can apply almost any style you want to almost any house, but the best styles match inside and out. So knowing the feel, tone and tempo you want for your house can help you pick both the style and have that style influence the size of rooms, the brightness and layout, etc.

The typical square footage for a family room is generally 18 x 18-square feet, or 18 x 20. That would be the size we would suggest you shoot for.

Master Bedroom

The master bedroom is the third major element of home design, and provides a wide opportunity of style, size and fixture choices. Here we have a variety of choices to make, such as size and style, of course, but also widow treatment, closet size, flooring, etc.

Do you want a walk-out balcony? A parlor or sitting area? Built in fixtures or flat walls? High arches or ceilings, slanted, low or cathedral? People spend a lot of time in their bedrooms and, like the family kitchen, tend to take a lot of time planning this room out to be both comfortable and personal.

When it comes to size, most of our master bedrooms come in at 13 x 14-square feet. That is our default measurement and the standard by which we go, with the understanding that making the master bedroom bigger or smaller will generally affect the size of adjoining or connecting rooms.

Master Bath

The fourth and final major element of home design is the master bathroom. Again, like the relationship between the family room and the kitchen, the choices you make with your master bedroom will affect your master bathroom.

The larger your sitting area or walk-in closet, for instance, the smaller your master bathroom might have to be. Or do you want the master bath in the front of the suite, to the side or in the back?

Our designers will help you see all of the facets, options and opportunities involved in your choices, and perhaps help you reach compromises that allow you to have the best of both worlds when it comes to your master bedroom and master bath.

When it comes to designing the master bathroom, there are other considerations to make as well. Do you want the master bath to be just for the master bedroom, so that the flow is quite organic from one room to the next? Do you want the master bath next to the master bedroom? Do you want the master bath to join two rooms, equally accessible to both, in what is known as a "Hollywood" or "Jack and Jill" style? Again, it's like a puzzle; the choices you make for this room will affect other rooms, and so require careful consideration and lots of visualization!

I always say, if you're going to scrimp on certain elements of the house, never scrimp on these main four elements; kitchen, family room, master bedroom and master bathroom. There are four main elements for a reason; because this is where, traditionally, home owners spend the most of their time.

In fact, when we begin to design a custom home for our clients we not only start with these four elements but really try to "wow" future homeowners with our designs for these four areas. If you can't get clients excited about their kitchen, family room, master bedroom or bath, how in the world can you hope to get them excited about the guest room or garage?

It's Not Just You: Designing for Resale

National averages reveal that most Americans live in their home for an average of seven years before moving out and moving on. While that's not something you want to dwell on as you invest precious time, energy and financial resources to the design of your new home, it is something to consider in the design of that home.

You will want to create a design that's not just attractive or comfortable to you, but that will appeal to potential buyers as well. We love to encourage our clients to be as personal, unique and inventive as possible when it comes to designing their homes, but not so unique that they'll be the only ones to ever be able to live in it!

That's why we try to blend the best of what we know, and families' love, with what each specific client brings to the home design process, as well. Once again, this gives them the best of both worlds; ideal living conditions while they own the house and optimal resale value, if and when, they ever decide to sell.

Chapter 4:
Advanced Home Design

Frank Lloyd Wright once said, "All good architectural design is a compromise." Only in the movies, with fancy special effects or in particular animation, can a truly compromise-free home exist. The rest of us have to deal with the physical limits of technology, space, opportunity, materials, and location, location, location.

Even if it's a multi-million dollar home belonging to Bill Gates or Tiger Woods, there is always compromise. For instance, you can't build on a mountain and expect oceanfront property, or vice versa. You can't build your dream home in the tropics and expect a white Christmas view outside your floor to ceiling picture window. You can't build on the Las Vegas strip and expect privacy, or even quiet.

For the rest of us mere mortals, compromise is even more expected. Now, you may be thinking to yourself,

"Well, Tim, the whole reason I'm building a custom home to begin with is because I don't want to compromise."

And you're right. But so am I. For instance, you may end up planning and building a single story home of your dreams, but it's not a two-story home, is it? If you ultimately decide to put your master bedroom on the ground floor of a two-story, then it can't be up. So, at some point in the planning process, you did compromise.

Most often you compromised in favor of a more attractive layout, or features, or less upkeep or simply a lower price. But there was a compromise. The key was making you happy about the compromise and hoping it turns out as a win-win.

Part of making compromises in your favor is finding a reputable, professional, experienced and expert Design/Build firm, like Whitestone Custom Homes. Ltd®. If you can find such a firm, trust them, believe in them, work with them and rely on them and you will be already halfway there.

In this chapter, we're going to discuss Advance Home Design, but don't worry, you won't need a drafting table of HVAC degree to understand it! What I mean by "advanced" is simply moving beyond the mere aesthetics of the home – although those are still important – to something we call "designing for cost."

Designing for Cost

After the concierge forms have all been filled out, the dreams turned into something more and more resembling reality, our design firm can begin creating what we call "working drawings." These begin to flesh out the actual design of your house, in language that contractors and building professionals can understand.

At this stage, we can begin to put the cost of the home into clearer focus for you, going room by room to determine what each team will be responsible for, providing estimates and blending it all together on a cost-by-cost basis.

Our goal in the working drawings is to create a balanced design that blends what you want and need with what is realistic in terms of your budget, lot-size, materials, projected costs, etc. In this, we strive to meet what we call "a majority" of your needs. We'd love to get you everything you want and even everything you need, within reason.

It is the "within reason" where compromise is typically necessary. Then again, if compromise is good enough for Bill Gates, Tiger Woods and Frank Lloyd Wright, well, we all should feel a little better about that by now, shouldn't we?

Price as You Go: Designing by Cost

As we go through the design process, we price the buyer's ideas out before we draw them. This way you have a much better idea of what each room, bell, whistle, square foot, tile or window treatment is going to cost you before we start talking to subcontractors, vendors and the like.

This is a far superior process than that used by most home builders, who design the home of your dreams with no calculator in sight, only to come back with a shocking price tag once all those pie in the sky designs are bid and tabulated.

This way you know throughout the process why compromise is so important and, critically, where compromises need to be made. When you know, for instance, how much that walk-in closet you've seen on Beverly Hills Housewives is going to cost and how it might be putting your husband's "man cave" in jeopardy, well, it's better to know that up front and make some compromises in the design of both, rather than get blindsided when the price comes in AFTER the working drawings are presented to subcontractors and vendors.

This way you can perhaps build a smaller closet and a smaller man cave and get what you both want; a compromise, I think, we can all be happy with.

Picture It As You Go: Crude by Design

One thing that's important to remember as we move through the advance home design process is that these initial working drawings won't include elevation.

In fact, sometimes they may look downright crude, hence the term "working" drawings instead of "final" drawings. The industry term for this is a "cartoon" or a "blocked out" plan.

These working drawings are not necessarily for you to show off to your friends, but rather, to move the process along to the advanced stage and provide subcontractors and vendors with a design so they can begin looking at square footage and what that might cost.

How Your House Gets So Expensive: Foot by Foot

If you're wondering how a few thousand square feet turns into a few hundred thousand dollars, well, you're in luck! In this section of advanced home design, I'll walk you through a few of the ways in which your crude "working drawing" can reveal how expensive each room might be:

Square feet

In as much as a butcher charges by the pound and a boutique salon sells perfume by the ounce, the construction industry runs on square footage. In short, every foot costs something, and many/most of the vendors and trade craftsmen bid by the square foot.

Most people only consider the square footage that is "under air." That is, with a roof over it and living space treated by air conditioning. The construction industry has a variety of ways of measuring a square foot that includes under air and then some.

For instance, a "framer" charges by what is called "covered" square footage. That includes all living areas, the garage, the overhangs and the porches. As one might imagine, when charging by the foot, this can add up quickly. Additionally, you must consider the square footage of big porches and other outdoor living area. In fact, many homebuilders calculate the square footage of those areas when they tell you how big the home is. The same is true for garages. That is part of the calculation that must be included. Some Builders even calculate the interior cubic air footage. All that open space comes at some cost.

Plumbing

Another expense that can add up quickly is plumbing, which may seem like it only exists in the bathroom and under sinks, but in fact can snake through the entire house when you consider how water gets to your upstairs bathroom.

Cabinets!

You wouldn't imagine that cabinet space could drive up the cost of a home, but you'd be surprised. Depending on the type of cabinets you select, how many of them, upper and lower and what kind of finish, you'd be amazed by how much that affects the cost of your kitchen.

Every foot of cabinet goes up in cost depending on the finish, the model, the make or the quality of material involved. It seems like such a minor thing when you're talking about floor tiles and an outdoor living room, but look to how many square feet of cabinets you're planning on having and how that affects the bottom line kitchen cost.

This is why both the concierge form and the working drawing are so important when it comes to making compromises. Room by room, we can point to the hidden costs that drive up the final estimate and, in this way, they can be addressed instance by instance.

Obviously, this isn't my first time at the rodeo, nor is it my sales team's. So, as we discuss the concierge form with clients, we might point out that a certain finish of cabinet can get exorbitant, hard to find, etc. This can help avoid surprises later, but even then, it often takes the working drawing estimates to make those prices clear for home builders.

Complexity

The more complex your home design, the more bells and whistles you include on your concierge form – Tuscan elevation, a lot of closet space, gourmet serving island, two dishwashers, built in cabinets, double stair cases, epoxy floor covering in the garage, etc. – the more expensive it is.

When we're talking about walk in closets, man caves, arboretums and speakers in the garage, this probably shouldn't come as a surprise, but it often does, and so I want to address that here momentarily.

The term most related to complexity in the construction industry is *Aspect Ratio*. Simply put, a low aspect ratio home is a less expensive home, while a high aspect ratio home costs more. For instance, your typical suburban square or rectangular home, which from the air might look like a gift box or shoebox shaped home, has a low aspect ratio. Why? Because it's simply less complex than other styles of home.

Now, compare that box-shaped, low-aspect ratio home with one that is wrapped around a swimming pool in a central courtyard, with cupolas coming out of the roof and multiple exits and levels, and the aspect ratio goes higher and higher with each design flourish.

So, while the more complex home is beautiful, it should come as no surprise that, with such complexity, comes a higher price tag.

Porches

It's great to sit on your covered, screened-in porch at the end of a long day and kick back with a refreshing drink and the joy of custom home ownership. And while covered porches aren't as expensive as, say, an air-conditioned and interior room, they're more expensive than most home buyers realize.

Fancy Interior finishing

The fancy flourishes that clients love to decorate their interiors with, such as trim, crown molding, tiled ceilings or inlaid tile walls and faux panting, those interior finishes add up. Room by room, square foot by square foot, we provide a variety of options if this is where home builders want to eventually compromise.

Parting Words: Nothing Is Ever Perfect

It's a fact of life that no matter how fully you participated in this advanced home design, no matter how long it took or active you were or how fully your envisioned the final product, one day you'll look up at your finished home and think how you might have changed something.

It could be your first week in the home, a year or two later or ten years down the road, but at some point you'll reconsider a design flourish, an angle, a room or a feature and experience, if not buyer's remorse, then the slight sting of "could have been."

This is the reason I don't recommend that perfectionists build custom homes; they experience this tenfold and twice as rapidly! But, if you know going in that, as Frank Lloyd Wright so tactfully put it, "All good architectural design is a compromise," then you can experience those moments of "would have done, should have done, could have done" with less regret.

The reason we at Whitestone Custom Homes spend so much time in the planning, development and design/advance design phase is because we want you to be fully prepared for the entire process; before, during and after construction. The more you know going in, we like to say, the less regret you'll have *moving* in!

Chapter 5:
The Colors of Your Life

If you think about it, color is a fairly significant part of your new home design. Not just the exterior of your home, but in particular, the interior. Look around any home, look around *your* home, and you'll quickly see that every room needs a color.

The pink polka dots in your daughter's room, the blue cloud cover on your son's ceiling, the earthy tones of your living room and the decorative glass tile backsplash in your kitchen, all bring life to otherwise what could be lackluster living space. Even the absence of color is a decision one must make when designing their new custom home.

As you might imagine, the more rooms you have to design, the more stressful all of these color choices become. This chapter is designed to help alleviate that stress and give you some background into why color is so important, and how to make wise choices with the help of a professional designer.

The Designer Touch: Bringing Your Style to Life

By the time you're ready to make choices about the colors for various room interiors, the building blocks are all pretty much in place. You've got the rest of the home down cold; square footage, room design, layout, what goes where, why and how it all fits together – it's all in place.

Now you're at a point where it's time to layer on the details that will turn the building blocks of a house into a comfortable, livable, new dream home. Believe it or not, color is a huge part of that.

In my experience, most people who are ready to build a new custom home are already fairly savvy about their own personal style. They're at an age where they may have owned, and decorated, several homes already, so they know how to match throw pillows to couches to wall art to window dressing.

And yet, designing a new custom home gives them the opportunity to try new things, to experiment with different, maybe bolder, colors and to get current. At Whitestone Custom Homes we have access to all the latest designs, color blends, combinations and textures to help new homeowners take advantage of the latest, greatest designs available.

Picking the colors of your home is a lot like becoming a new bride. By that I mean, what's the first thing a newly engaged woman does before planning her big day? That's right, she goes out and buys every bridal magazine on the newsstand.

Likewise, before building a custom home, most future homeowners rush out and snatch up every back copy of *Home and Design* and *Architectural Design* they can find.

Inside, they'll find all kinds of current and modern aspects they'd like to add to their homes, and we encourage them to begin creating "scrapbooks" of their favorite design features and bring them in when meeting with our trained, professional designers.

It's amazing to me to see how far we've evolved in home design, especially since I can remember a time not so long ago when every new home owner seemed to want one of two colors; forest green and harvest gold!

Today, of course, homeowners have such a wide range of colors to choose from: from linen white to kangaroo, from glowing apricot to dill weed, from gray wisp to Kennebunkport green, and textures and accessories, as well. At Whitestone Custom Homes we often use tile, wood or other accents to accent a wall color and living up a room.

Wallpaper keeps trying to make a comeback, but with so many modern paint and texture offerings on the market these days, it's been a challenge for that industry to make a comeback. Still, we like to provide our clients with all the options that might appeal to them, so our library is both wide and deep.

Professional Help Makes All the Difference

What we do at Whitestone Custom Homes is pair you with a professional interior designer to bring your ideas to life. The issue of color can seem to be underwhelming, a simple no-brainer. That is, until you're faced with the latest, greatest choices. That's when things get difficult.

What our decorators do is determine, through a series of exercises and worksheets, what your personal color style is. For instance, my decorator tells me I'm a "shade of gray," and looking around my home and office, I can see that shades in the gray family are certainly a factor in my design choices. So when it's time to design a model home, she'll often factor in gray knowing I'll like it, and assuming other people will as well.

But every family brings its own style and sensibility to a project. Some are in the yellow or red family, others in the brown or beige, while some are autumn, some winter, some summer and some spring. Just knowing your color wheel is only half the battle, though.

Many clients come into the design center with a vague idea of what colors they want to see, but falter when it comes to pinning them down. That's where a design professional like our trained interior decorators come in handy.

It's easy enough to get advice from friends and family, or even folks who've just gone through the design process and know what to expect. But, they're not you and you're not them. This is your house, your design and it's not exactly cheap, so why not take the time to sit with a professional and do it right the first time?

What do I mean by a professional? Our interior decorators practice their craft on a regular basis, on a current basis and are professionally trained to do so for a living. They're an outside source, a fresh pair of eyes, and an objective ally in taking your ideas and making them a reality in ways you may not have ever imagined or even contemplated for.

I'm not just talking about the creative aspects of interior design but the practical aspects of basic home and color design. Seeing a color scheme on paper is one thing, but we all know that what looks good on paper doesn't always translate to real life.

Installing a color scheme in real time, in a real home, kitchen or bath, making mistakes or misfires and learning from them, is critical to the professional experience our designers bring to new home design.

Fear x Excitement = Transformation

When choosing the colors for a custom home, you can't eliminate the emotional aspect of what those colors mean to people. I called this chapter "The Colors of Your Life" for a reason; your home is central to your life and the colors you choose during the design phase are going to be the ones you look at, touch, see and feel for many years to come.

So they better be right, and they better be right the first time, because it's not cheap to re-do. So at Whitestone Custom Homes we use a basic emotional formula in all the design and prep work we do:

<u>Fear x Excitement = Transformation</u>

There is a good amount of fear around home design, because once it comes out of your head and onto a concierge form, and later a blueprint and a floor plan, a working plan and a foundation, walls and a roof, it becomes real. And reality is pretty scary stuff, particularly if you've dreamed of your dream home, as many clients do, for years and years.

There is just something about committing to a design decision, particularly around color, that makes folks fearful. Our designers walk you through the equation to take you from fear to excitement and from excitement to transformation.

Building a new home is a transformation, make no mistake. You will be transforming your life; not just your address or square footage, but how you live. We work hard to build more than houses, but custom homes--places a family live, work, eat, laugh and play. That deserves nothing less than our best professional effort and your full cooperation.

That's why we encourage you to share with us your design ideas. Keep tearing out those magazine pages, printing off website graphics, or even driving around the neighborhood and going to visit model homes and snapping pictures with your cell phone or digital camera. Share them with us so we can help you personalize your style and make it a reality.

Be Aware of Current Trends

Naturally, custom home design goes through periodic changes and upgrades, just like any other industry. Every three months or so, it seems, we can see a subtle trend or nuance emerge, seemingly out of nowhere.

An accessory or flourish or design tweak that suddenly becomes a part of the design flow that starts to occur throughout the industry. A new color scheme or stripes are suddenly in vogue. Bigger changes come every year or so and major changes happen every three years or so. Trends come and go, like forest green and harvest gold.

I can remember years ago when stainless steel was actually regarded as "low end" in new homes, while today it's the gold standard in appliances and what everybody wants. Once upon a time, polished brass was what everybody clamored for, now it's a style of industrial steel that seems so popular.

These trends change on a regular basis and it's our job to keep up with those changes, but also emphasize the classic design features, choices and options that seem to defy trends, fads and phases.

Keeping It In House

Other custom home designers use a variety of contractors at any one time, so that when it comes time to make both design choices and purchases, the homeowner has to go to this appliance store and that tile store, from this interior decorator's showroom to an electrical shop or a lighting shop or a furniture showroom.

What we've done is provide solutions, not problems. We know what our customers want; yesterday, today and tomorrow. We stay current and focused, not just on design trends but customer needs. We know you don't want to run around and do all this yourself- that's why we do it for you.

Our designers know where to look when you want something special, unique, or out of the way. They combine creativity with practicality in securing what you need when you need it, and offering design advice throughout the process.

Under one roof, we hammer out the problems and provide solutions so that you don't have to go to fifteen places just to finish your living room, then fifteen more for the kitchen and so on.

All creativity needs guardrails. We talked earlier in this book about the "kid in a candy shop" mentality that many homeowners feel when faced with endless choices.

The Whitestone custom design process involves narrowing your choices based on your style, color scheme, personality and needs so that you can make wiser choices faster, and better, with our professional guidance. It's not about limitation so much as avoiding confusion, intimidation, and getting "frozen" for fear of making the wrong choices simply because there are so many choices.

It's really important to feel confident in your decision making process, and that's why we work closely with you to empower you to make your own choices based on a particular palette or array of widely available materials, designs, colors, fabrics, accessories and options. If you don't feel confident about your choices, you won't feel confident – or happy – about the home you're building.

And what's the point of that? When you have to run around to ten or twelve or fifteen different vendors choosing hardware and tile, backsplashes, ceiling fans and flooring, you may hear a different viewpoint from each vendor, leaving you confused and distrustful of your original design team. It won't necessarily mean that those vendors aren't right, but… are they right for you?

The reason we assign each family a seasoned, experienced, veteran and professional interior designer is to spend the time, energy and creativity to get to know you, your style, your wants, your needs and then take that knowledge to design the most personal, the most current, the most beautiful home with the latest materials. That's the personal touch you can't find from a dozen varying opinions from relative strangers.

Color Choice: A Two-Part Process

We generally separate the task of color design into two specific parts, "DECO A" and "DECO B," and both involve making real-time choices in a three-dimensional world. The first part, DECO A, would include cabinets, basic plumbing, fixtures, countertops, exterior colors, as well as both exterior and interior masonry. We typically hold the flooring choices until later, so for us this first step is really about getting the client comfortable with the basics of color design.

The next step, DECO B, comes a little later, once the framing of the house is up and clients can actually come in and walk through and see how their design choices are literally coming to life. This is a really fun time for clients because we bring back their personal interior decorator, and with an entire framed out house around them, they can literally look at the choices available in real time together.

In the past, we used to make all the color and design choices in one step, at the beginning of the process, but we learned through experience that doing it this way makes the whole process easier for our customers. So now we've learned from experience – there's that word again – that leaving some design and color choices until Phase 2 really helps to show the clients what their decisions will look in real time and, thus, cut down on (costly) mistakes. Sometimes, with the type of loan you have, we pick all the decorator selections up front before we start the home. Those details can be discussed with your sales person.

The process continues until you sign off on both steps of the process with forms called DECOA "Final" and DECO B "Final," meaning your choices are made, you've understood the process, are happy with those decisions and have essentially signed off on them once and for all.

The reason we use the word "final" on those two DECO forms is because it is my strong and personal recommendation that clients not make any changes after filling out both those forms. It's easy to second guess oneself and wake up in the middle of the night certain you should change the backsplash in the bathroom to lemongrass instead of Kennebunkport green, but trust me...second guesses are like potato chips, you can't have just one!

One second guess leads to another and another until your confidence is shaken and you're concerned that none of the choices you made were right. But in my experience, and for 99.9 percent of my clients, the first choice was usually the best – and for good reason.

Remember, those earlier, wiser choices were made with the assistance of a highly-trained design professional, while those late night or early morning second guesses were made on your own, with no assistance our outside help, or even a buffer to help you fine tune them. They were also made in concert with a lot of other color choices, to help "blend" the interior home design as one.

Oftentimes, changing one element of the color wheel, willy-nilly and at the last minute, is like pulling a thread and unraveling half the sweater. Instead, it's best to stick to the original design, watch it come to life and appreciate the time, energy and effort that went into pulling it all together.

Parting Words: The Colors of Your Life

I can't stress enough the importance of carefully choosing the color scheme of your new custom home. These truly are "the colors of your life," because regardless of how hard you work, live, earn or play, home is still where you spend the majority of your time.

While picking colors may seem like a "no brainer" and hardly worth devoting an entire chapter to, I hope by now you can see how much work goes into laying out the color scheme of every room in your home. From bathroom to bedroom and kitchen to den and every nook, cranny, ledge and surface in between, it's never too early to start thinking about the colors you'll be enjoying for the "life" of your new home.

Chapter 6:
The Construction Phase

The construction phase is obviously quite critical to the completion of your dream custom home, but you don't necessarily have to wear a hard hat to get in on the act.

The good news is, that for you, by the time we enter the construction phase, your hard work is mostly over. You've participated in the planning phases, through conception and design, making hard choices about how to accessorize and even color each room inside and outside your house.

Now it's time to see those plans become a reality. Don't get me wrong, we still want – and need – your partnership through every phase of the process. The only difference is that now we kind of take the "handoff" and run with the ball to the end zone.

Believe it or not, my feeling on the construction phase is that it should be relatively easy and positively fun. This is where the rubber meets the road, so to speak, where all your clippings and webpage links and home design magazine cutouts come to life, where all those forms you filled out, boxes you checked and decisions you've made, come to life.

We want to take as much of the work off your hands as possible while still letting you enjoying seeing each phase of the construction process develop.

The Process of Discovery: Your New Hobby?!?

I never forget that, for most people, building their dream home is the largest single purchase in their life. I know how daunting it can be, from visualizing that dream home, to conceptualizing it, to planning it and framing it out to, naturally, paying for it.

I call that whole process the "process of discovery," and it truly is awe-inspiring to watch the faces of satisfied clients as they experience it for themselves.

What I find with most clients as that they begin this process of discovery is that they get hooked on it. Much like they got addicted to taking model home tours and scrapbooking living room designs or wall colors during the planning phase, during the construction phase they likewise get hooked on seeing each day's progress.

Imagine driving up to the work site, seeing a wall that wasn't there yesterday, a hill that used to be a flat patch of land, a window or a door that wasn't there before.

Our hobbies are those things we do in our spare time, at night when we get home from work, or on the weekends or over the holidays; gardening, stamp collecting, reading or going to the movies. For many new home builders/ home buyers, watching the construction phase becomes their new hobby, and with good reason. Few things can rival the feeling of watching a home – especially your new custom home – being built from the ground up.

And, unlike a hobby such as watching TV, going to the library or sitting in a movie theater, there is some action to the construction phase. You're there, in the fresh air, seeing the day's developments live and in person. There's an active element to it, like gardening, where you're participating in the birth, and growth, of a living thing. We love it, but please be very careful around a job site.

The equation I shared with you last chapter--***Fear + Excitement = Transformation***--applies here, as well. There is naturally some fear, or at least concern, as the construction phase begins. The permits are all in order, the lot is buzzing with activity, and contractors are coming and going in their work trucks. But, the fear slowly turns into excitement as the foundation is laid, walls go up and activity increases. And finally, transformation--from blueprints, permits, hard hats and an empty lot to a home. Not just any home, your home; your dream home.

If watching that happen isn't a worthy hobby, then I don't know what is!

Understanding the Construction Process

Regardless of which builder you use, I want you to understand the construction process so that you can have clarity and confidence in your custom home builder. Informed home owners are happy home owners, and the more you know about the process, I believe, the more you'll enjoy it.

The process begins with your participation. The more you behave as a partner, the more you'll understand and take away from the construction of your new home. We want you there throughout the construction phase, watching and observing, not just standing outside the fence looking on from a distance. This helps us build with confidence and you enjoy the process so much more.

What's unique about Whitestone Custom Homes is our clientele. In our price range, at our level of sophistication, our clients are already creative, passionate, talented, successful, motivated and ambitious people. They generally understand when walking into our showroom that they're going to be building a $300,000 to $900,000 home and are more than ready to do that. You don't get to that level without achieving some form of success in your life, and we recognize, appreciate, and honor that fact.

Likewise, you recognize, appreciate and honor the fact that I'm going to provide over three decades of experience to deliver a custom home that doesn't just meet your expectations, but exceeds it. All the trials and errors of my career, every home I've built, with my hands or for another builder or with Whitestone, has taught me invaluable lessons that, frankly, takes several decades or more to thoroughly understand.

You are now part of that process. And it is a process. It's a process because we've learned that's what works best: A formula, a plan and a system that builds on every past customer's needs and has refined them into a repeatable, transferable process that we can use to deliver your custom home with confidence and expertise.

Understanding also leads to fewer challenges and, frankly, arguments along the way. We recognize that building a home, while fun, is not without its challenges. When you understand the process fully, you can sleep better at night and avoid arguments with your spouse and family that might arise from a lack of understanding.

Clear deadlines and deliverables, progress reports and summaries, these are all part of helping our clients understand not only the process itself, but where we are along the trajectory of that process so they can breathe, and sleep, easier!

There's nothing worse than spending a lot of time, energy and effort on a project and, through lack of understanding, finding it less than satisfactory as it plays out in reality. We want your home to be a peaceful, relaxing, comforting, fun place to live. Not just the new custom home you're building, but the old home you're still living in while it's being built. That can't happen when you're frustrated, and one thing that leads to frustration is a general lack of knowledge or understanding about something you're going through.

Step by Step Home Design: The Construction Phase

Once the design and decorating processes are complete, it's time to begin the construction phase:

Step 1: *PHR # 1*

The first step in this process is something known as the PHR # 1 Form. PHR stands for Purchaser Home Review, and you'll see why in a moment.

This form is used when you, as the client, meet with the construction personnel to determine where exactly the home will fit on the site. Should it be dead center, a little off to the left, the right, etc.?

Once that's determined, you'll move offsite to the office or perhaps a nearby model home and sit down to review various aspects of the PHR #1 Form. This helps clarify for the construction personnel any lingering questions or last minute opportunities or clarifications. It's also an opportunity for the sales team you've been working with to kind of "hand off" the next phase to construction.

Step 2: *PHR # 2*

Once the construction personnel have reviewed all the plans, designs and change orders, it's time to move on to Step 2 of the construction process. The Purchaser Home Review # 2 Form is the foundation of this next step, and is basically the formal document that you, construction, and the sales staff sign off on to make the handoff from sales to construction final.

This process will ensure that all the hours of careful planning you did with the sales and design staff are included and communicated to the construction manager, who is the person ultimately responsible for the completion of your custom home.

These two forms, the Purchaser Home Review # 1 and Purchaser Home Review # 2, are the perfect opportunity to bring the construction manager up to speed, with your full involvement and the sales and design staff's support, and then take that ball and run with it. You're not building the home, neither are sales or design. The Construction Manager is, and so these forms help bring him or her up to speed with your full involvement.

It's also a good opportunity for you to become acquainted with your Construction Manager, to communicate any overarching concerns or challenges you may be facing and ask questions about the construction phase the sales or design team might not have been able to answer, or answer to your satisfaction.

Get It in Writing!

These two forms are also a kind of formal step for you to get your wishes in writing. This is the same advice I'd give my parents, my siblings, my spouse, children or best friend- get it in writing. If you are absolutely, positively sure you want a feature in your home, get it in writing.

At Whitestone homes, it's not so much an issue of trust that you formalize your wishes, but simply a bit of protocol to insure that everyone is on the same page.

As you might imagine, building a home is a complex, challenging and multi-faceted process with many, many people involved. The more complex a process, the more opportunities for errors exist. So, the more formal an agreement, a form or a desire becomes, the more certain you can be that it will survive the chain of command that must exist on a typical construction site.

. If I buy a new car, even one tricked out with all the latest bells and whistles, I may have a maximum of one or two conversations with the salesman and, boom, I'm out the door and heading on down the road. The conversations that surround building a new custom home are multiple and complex and involve various "teams" of people, from sales to design to decorating through construction. All totaled, you may wind up having 25, 50, 100 or more conversations with dozens of people with our team throughout the planning, design and construction phases. This doesn't count the number of conversations with your spouse, friends and relatives.

The more conversations you have with more people, the greater the likelihood that some tiny detail will get lost along the way. It's human nature, and frankly, unavoidable. But, putting the gist of those conversations in writing, as part of a written (versus merely verbal) plan, the work and change orders and these two new forms we've just introduced, insure that you get what you want simply because the construction personnel know to give it to you. How do they know? Because it's right there in writing, on some form, work order or punch list.

That's why, at Whitestone Custom Homes Ltd.®, our process is fairly involved and interactive. We want to give you ample opportunity to fully verbalize your vision for your home and work with us to create that reality, through various forms and plans and checklists.

Naturally, we want you to build with us. But, whoever you build with, make sure to get the details in writing so that your dream home doesn't turn into a nightmare.

We've talked about clarity throughout the design and decorating phases, and now I'll bring it up again when it comes to construction; the clearer your goals, wishes, and desires, the more likely that is to be translated into your new custom home.

The forms, plans, and procedures that make up this process are vital for not only clarity, but understanding your vision. Just as when I sat down to write this book, I couldn't just start on page one and write until I was finished. It took a lot of careful planning, organizing and conceptualizing to accomplish the reality of what I pictured in my mind when the idea first occurred to me.

Building a home should be no different.

Step 3: *PHR # 3*

Once the first two forms are signed off on, construction formally begins. The work starts and crews arrive and progress continues until about the time we get to the sheet rock phase, at which time we have another formal meeting to complete the Purchaser Home Review # 3 Form.

This is a good opportunity to continue refining the construction of your home, a "refresher" for you to sit down – or actually walk through the home – with the construction manager and ensure that the home is according to plan. If not, it's better to catch minor changes at the sheetrock phase than later, when fixes become more involved, costly, and in some cases, impossible.

This is also a good opportunity to get more clarity around the specifics of various home accessories you may have ordered, such as where to put speakers, security systems, media integration, such as iPods and iPhones, etc.

Once you've signed off on the PHR # 3 Form, the process picks up again. Here we'll begin installing the various cabinetry, fixtures and features you've selected at the Design Center.

Next will come those "Colors of Your Life," as we discussed in the last chapter, and with each brush of paint or splash of color the house truly does become a home. Meanwhile, things are proceeding at pace as the finishing touches are installed, from tile and backsplashes, wood accents, carpeting, etc.

Beware the "Ugly Duckling" Phase

Every home, no matter how gorgeous, perfect and "dreamy" it winds up, goes through what I call the "ugly duckling" stage first. It may only last a day or two, but here you come, ready to inspect the process and it all looks so scattered and half-baked, wiring exposed, plastic wrapping bunched on the floor, paint the wrong color because it's not really paint but merely primer, and if you're not prepared for it, you can go home feeling fairly discouraged.

You wonder how it will ever come together. Well, trust me, it comes together. I guarantee you that every inventory home, and definitely all our model homes, that you've ever ooh'd and aah'd about, went through an ugly duckling phase before the last slip cover, throw pillow, backsplash and blind was in place.

Your home will be no different.

Mistakes Are There to Be Fixed

It's uncommon to complete a home without at least a few mistakes, but the promise of Whitestone Custom Homes is that we're there to fix them. We don't put all that forethought and planning into the design and decorating of the home only to flub the job in the construction phase.

Every mistake can be fixed, and our team of highly trained, professional and courteous construction personnel is there to fix them for you to your ultimate satisfaction.

Step 4: *PHR # 4*

Once the home is complete, we get to the Purchaser Home Review # 4 Form, or PHR # 4 Form. This is an exciting time for us, and for you, because it's basically our formal "introduction" to the home. While walking you through your new home, we go down a variety of checklists and forms to make sure you understand all of your home features.

From big to small, from functional to sexy, we want you to know how your house works:

- **Where do you find the emergency water cutoff?**
- **Where are the water heaters and how do you drain them?**
- **How does the Sprinkler System work?**
- **Where is the emergency shutoff button for the garage door?**

- **Where are all the thermostats and how do they work?**
- **Where are all the warranties for each of the appliances?**

We'll walk through all of these with you, answering any questions you may have, and frequently, many you never thought to ask. Room by room, we will make sure there are no discrepancies, no unfinished business and, if there are, we'll put them on a "punch," or to do, list and ensure that they are resolved to your satisfaction.

When they are, you'll sign off on your fourth and final form, the Purchaser Home Review # 4 Form, and that's that- you are now the proud owner of a custom dream home!

Chapter 7:
Mortgage, Closing Decisions and Title Companies

I know more about mortgages than I ever thought I would, mainly because we do very little cash over the barrel head homes. Instead, 99 percent of our clients use mortgages, and over the years, you begin to pick up a thing or two.

This chapter is designed to help you understand your mortgage, closing decisions and title companies based on my almost thirty years of dealing with them.

Experience Comes With Practice

The one thing you don't want to trust your new custom home mortgage to is inexperience. As I stated in the last chapter, a custom home is often one of the client's biggest purchases in life, and you don't want inexperience to throw a monkey wrench in the process.

Instead, you want to deal with people who are doing mortgages, and only mortgages, every day, for a living.

Oftentimes, a client will come to us and want to use their own mortgage provider, but we prefer to work with one preferred lender because we know he knows what it takes to get the job done, on time, with all the i's dotted and t's crossed.

Not only do we work with them on a regular basis, but they also specialize in new home loans, and *only* new home loans. They're not sitting at a bank desk handling car loans in the morning and boat loans in the afternoon and condo loans the next morning and motorcycle loans in the evening, and look, finally a home loan comes across their desk.

Why is this so important to us? The fact is, new home loans are different than other types of loans, even used home loans and especially car, motor home, trailer home, commercial building or motorcycle loans. Rather than someone who does all kinds of loans but is expert at none, we prefer to deal with someone who is an expert at new home loans.

This helps us eliminate surprises, makes us confident that you'll get the best rate and broadens your options for different kinds of programs. What's nice about our preferred lender is that he's part of that overall team feeling you get at WhiteStone Custom Homes. This makes him not only part of the process, but part of a seamless process that you might not get with an outside lender who doesn't have that same "team" mentality, or even personal connection.

Obviously, we can't choose lenders for you. It will always be your option as to which lender you choose, but we highly suggest our preferred lender for the reasons listed above.

Fast, Good or Cheap, But Not All of the Above

The "designer's triangle" states that you can get something fast, good or cheap, but not all three. The same holds true for mortgages. So, for instance, if you're getting a really cheap rate, something is suffering on either the quality or expediency end. The rate may be being offered by a fly-by-night company or a company offering a "special deal." We call these mortgage companies a "Bubba Mortgage Company."

Ultimately, however, they're not part of the team and, if something goes wrong with the loan they'll inevitably blame it on the home builder, not themselves. It can lead to petty squabbles or even blown deals, and we never like to see that happen to anyone.

Let's say you want to at least "price" or "term" shop and are looking for an outside lender, where would you start? I always suggest the internet. There are a lot of great apps for finding mortgage rates, terms, loan durations, and the like, that will work like a breeze when you type in the parameters of your search, such as how much you're looking to borrow, for how long and your ideal interest rate.

Making a Commitment

When you find a mortgage company that fits your needs, what next? Well, when you're working with

WhiteStone Custom Homes, we ask that you go to your loan officer and get what is called a "commitment" loan.

A commitment letter is different than an opinion letter or credit approval. Those may be fine for used or existing homes, but building a custom home takes a larger commitment and we actually require the more formal commitment letter over a simple credit approval.

Why we insist on this is because we have to take that commitment letter from your loan officer to our bank in order to borrow the money necessary to build your home for you.

This letter gives the bank confidence in the fact that someone wants to buy that home when we're done, i.e. we're not just building it on spec and hoping to sell it after it's finished.

Many people don't want to go through the process of getting an actual commitment letter because to do so requires the lender to check their credit, which may "ding" or affect their credit rating if enough people check it before obtaining the letter.

We fully understand and want to honor that fact. On the other hand, making a commitment is a big part of the home building process, for you and for us. If you're building a home with us or any builder, however, at some point you need to make a commitment regardless of your stellar credit rating.

Once you commit to getting the commitment letter, your lender will enter another, more critical phase of the lending process. Here, the company will need to get down to business, obtaining verification of employment, deposits of record, tax receipts, etc.

It's vital that, as the loan approaches, you begin to gather this material together, and there are many forms on the internet, most likely on your lender's website in particular, to help walk you through this.

Of course, getting a loan is never guaranteed. Regardless of your financial situation, now is the time to get good credit, make it better or keep it stable. I always tell prospective clients that now is *not* the time to go out and open up a bunch of credit cards, buy a new car or boat or otherwise "rock the boat" when it comes to your precious credit.

The loan is not entirely based on income, after all, but your ability to pay the mortgage loan in relation to various other factors, such as your income, outstanding debts, new debts, etc.

I know it can be tempting to rush out and buy a ton of new furniture, a new bed or master bedroom suite, massive grill, etc., in anticipation of moving into the house. But, wait until you get the financing set and in stone and then go out and splurge if you still want to. It may sound severe but I've seen many instances where people come in and see us, get excited about our model homes and design plans, get into initial talks with us, and in anticipation of working together, go out and charge massive amounts on new furniture for the home. But when a creditor sees that type of sudden and massive new activity on top of a $300,000 to $900,000 mortgage commitment, these folks have essentially disqualified themselves from the loan with their premature spending spree. Think about it before your home is built. You have put substantial deposits down and now you don't qualify for the home. It is not worth it, trust me.

What's more, it's not just the initial borrowing phase, but further on in the process that counts. As you might imagine, in our current economic client lenders are extremely cautious. Many insist on another credit review, or update, before the closing date, so if you go out and splurge during that time you could still put your loan at risk.

The current home lending climate is such that upon closing of your home loan, the lender may send out an appraiser to ensure the home is up to completion and code.

Closing Counts

As construction nears its end, about 45 days in advance of completion, our office will send you a letter posting an official, expected date when your home will be finished. As the date nears we get firmer and firmer about an actual date, and will update you on that, as well. This allows you to settle up issues with your current home, arrange for movers to come, pack your things, etc.

As far as your mortgage goes, you will have your closing at a title company. Now, we use the same title company all the time and for the very same reasons we like to use a preferred lender.

As part of our "team," this preferred title company can make sure all the documents are there, we know they'll work with us on scheduling and deadlines, they're proficient with the paperwork and, what's more, we trust them.

That's our job, actually, to find trusted vendors to help make your custom home a dream home, and that's why we work with so many people over and over again.

We like to work with people who know what they're doing, do it for a living and can be trusted, again and again, to do it well. That way you can worry about moving into your home, and we can worry about the details, including the title company.

At the end of the closing at the title company, the mortgage lender will fund the loan, and once the paperwork is signed, you'll get the keys to your new home. After that, the home is yours.

It's time to move in, and that just so happens to be the topic of our next chapter!

Chapter 8:
Moving In – And Living In – Your Home

There's nothing quite like moving into your own home. And, not just your own home, but your own new, entirely personalized, custom built dream home. I've watched proudly as many families took the keys from my hand and literally danced through the front doors of their house, ready to start living in the home they created and designed from scratch.

I'd be remiss if I told you that's the end of the story. Because to live "happily ever after" in your custom built home, you really want to educate yourself so that your home can deliver its peak potential.

I liken it to getting the latest iPhone and neglecting to read the instruction manual. How many applications would go unnoticed, how many features ignored, if you simply turned the phone on and started texting?

Likewise, your new custom built home is a finely turned machine waiting to deliver to its maximum potential, if only you'll hit the "pause" button for a few minutes to learn how all those fancy new bells and whistles work. So that's what we'll be doing in this, our final chapter together.

Conversational Facts versus Real Facts

One thing I've learned when it comes to homeowners, neighbors, families, friends, and people in general is that not only is everyone a critic, but everyone's an *expert*. The minute you take ownership of your home you will be privy to all this expertise, whether you want it or not!

A neighbor will tell you the twelve reasons why your foundation is cracked. An aunt will clue you in to the best way to run your dishwasher (run hot water first!) and your Dad will assure you of the best way to mow your lawn – or tune up your lawnmower. A coworker will insist you have a 12-digit code for your garage doors.

These are what are known as "conversational facts." In other words, people hear, say and share these "truisms" in conversation and so, after time, they sound like facts, but they aren't facts. Your aunt may truly believe that running hot water before starting the dishwasher will make it more effective, and perhaps it was in 1959. But today's dishwashers are carefully calibrated and finely tuned and running the water – hot or not – before starting a cycle won't have the least effect on how clean your dishes will be when they're dry.

My point here is that you've hired an expert to build your home, now listen to one as he explains how to move into your home with the least amount of hassle and the most effective solutions for a smooth transition.

I started in this business in customer service, taking complaints from all kinds of home owners about all types of home ownership issues. And now, owning my own business and walking proud new owners through their spiffy new homes, I know what to look for, what to warn them about and how to solve any minor – even major – issues that may arise.

In this chapter, I'll scroll through just a few high-level maintenance tips that will show you the quickest, easiest and simplest ways to avoid 99.9% of home maintenance issues. "Do it yourself" ads will try to scare you into thinking you need a dozen add-in warranties or workmen in your house every day to stave off mold, ammonia, radon leaks, sagging roofs, cracking foundations, peeling paint and 1,001 other potential problems. Like anything else, preventive maintenance is the key to disaster relief.

Follow me on a virtual tour of your new home – of any new home – and you'll see that, with a minimal amount of effort just a couple times a year, you and your home can get along just fine!

The Best Offense is a Good Defense

For most of us, our home is the biggest investment we'll ever make. Like any investment, it must be nurtured, tended, and above all, maintained. A lot of folks think that buying a custom home means that everything should be "plug and play" and since it's all brand new, they won't have to worry about it for the next 20 to 30 years.

Well, ideally, that's true but the fact is every home goes through a certain amount of wear and tear and with just some routine maintenance you can avoid costly breakdowns and even costlier repairs. Even a brand new car needs air in its tires from time to time, oil changes at certain increments and minor tune-ups occasionally. So, too, your house needs a little TLC from time to time. Yes, even your brand new, custom built dream home!

Home Maintenance 101: Top Tips for Maximum Home Performance

What are the highest priority items you need to do to keep your new home feeling, looking and performing just like it will on the day you move in? I'm glad you asked. Below you'll find half a dozen or more of what I call Home Success Criteria to keep your home looking, and acting, new for years after you move in:

Warranties

The first things you should check out in your new home are the warranties. Depending on the size and complexity of your new home, there will likely be a dozen or more such warranties on everything from the refrigerator and microwave to the speakers in the garage and to the washer and dryer in the laundry room.

We always put all your warranties in the same place in every home; the first drawer to the right of the dishwasher. Keep them there if you'd like. Make this your warranty drawer and examine each one closely. There will be address cards to fill out, registrations to update and if you do these the first week you move in, you can be assured that all your major appliances will be protected for as long as the warranties allow.

Many such companies offer extended warranties that must be filled out and mailed within the first 30-days of moving into the home, so it's critical that you act and act quickly in order to fully protect all your beautiful new and appliances.

Photographic Evidence

Whenever I get a new car, I pull it into the middle of my circular drive and take a picture of it on the first day I drive it home. It's nice to look at it and see that "brand new car" shine, and every so often I'll scroll through my photos of old cars to see how great they looked fresh off the showroom floor.

I always recommend that clients walk through their home that first week, snapping pictures of their new custom built home. They can take the photos with the house empty, and then furnished, and then fully decorated.

This is more than just an academic or emotional pursuit, or something for the kids' scrapbook in later years. These pictures can prove valuable if you ever experience some kind of home damage like from a storm, a blown water heater, air conditioning leak, fire or other such disaster. Insurance companies or manufacturers rely on such photographic evidence to determine how much damage is depicted in the after photographs than the "before" pictures.

Reminders

We live in a great age of technology where nearly every cell phone, laptop, tablet or PC comes with some kind of software or app to help us keep track of important dates. Such reminders will be helpful as you go about maintaining your new home.

For instance:

- **Set up a reminder so that every six months (if not sooner) you replace your A/C filter.** Each time you replace your filter, pour some bleach into your main air conditioning drain. The main drain is typically in your attic or upstairs, and consists of a ¾ inch PVC pipe with an open end. This drains condensation from humidity and runoff from your A/C unit, and can get moldy – or worse – if not properly maintained. A little bleach poured into the main drain each time you replace the A/C filter is just the ticket.

- **Remind yourself to replace your fire detector batteries once a year.** A lot of folks like to pick a holiday, like New Year's Day or a season, such as Daylight Savings Time, to remind them of such routine maintenance.

- **Be on alert for differential settlement.** The foundation is literally the bedrock of your home, and should be maintained as often – if not more – than any of your home's systems. Lawns, yards, dirt and grass under and around the foundation should be kept uniformly moist – not too moist, and not too dry – to avoid leakage, cracks or what is commonly known as "differential settlement" of the foundation. Even if such settlement doesn't crack or otherwise damage the foundation, over time it can cause doors to stick and other household nuisances.

- **Drain your water heater twice a year.** Another time-sensitive home success criterion is to drain your water heater every six months. You can look up online, or in your owner's manual, exactly how to do this, but basically you will want to turn the water heater off, hook up a hose to the spigot and drain it. This will help eliminate lime deposits that can damage your water heater and cause it to leak and even burst, creating massive damage since water heaters are generally central to a variety of rooms in the home.

- **Get on that grout.** We do a lot of tile, marble and other stone-based accents in our homes and as such use a lot of grout. Grout is great for affixing tiles and sealing those gaps between them, but be on alert for cracking, peeling or missing grout as you begin to use the sinks, bathrooms and showers where the majority of the grout in your home appears. Moisture behind grout can cause mildew and other problems in your walls, and I don't have to tell you how dangerous that can be in a home. If you notice grout peeling, cracking or missing, be sure to replace it quickly to avoid further damage and costly repairs down the line. (DAP brand from Home Depot works great if you follow the directions carefully.)

- **Careful about caulking.** Just like grout needs to be examined regularly, be sure to do a visual inspection of the outside of your home regularly – I suggest every six months, as well – to ensure that there are no gaps, cracked or missing caulk. As homes settle and are exposed to the daily elements, the caulk that keeps windows tightly sealed and the elements out can take a lot of abuse. By regularly checking the caulk around your home, you can tell when it's in need of repair and the more often you check it, the less likely the repairs are going to be costly or extensive.

Home ownership is an awesome opportunity and mature responsibility. You've been so careful about designing, building and investing in your new custom home. Now that you've moved in, keep the momentums going by taking care of that investment.

Parting Words about Moving in – And Living In – Your New Home

Few experiences are as positive as spending the first night in a new home, and even fewer match the special feeling of sleeping in your new, custom built home for the very first time.

Now that you're settled in, you can turn your attention to maintaining your home like the proud new homeowner(s) you are. I hope this chapter has given you a sampling of nearly a dozen of the top home success criteria I can think of.

But don't stop there! Building a custom designed dream home is one thing. Living in it is an opportunity to make it even dreamier for your children, for your future, or for resale.

Conclusion
Home Sweet Home

My hope is that this book will put you in a unique position in the marketplace. I know of no other book that provides this detailed process for a quality home with a successful process as the one I've just shared with you.

If you read this book and apply its principles, you are going to have an unfair advantage over other home buying customers, as well as new homeowners. You will be armed with the tools you need to build, care for, maintain, and either own or sell your new custom designed home.

So, what now? Well, you've finished the book. You've also finished your new custom home. You have just about everything you wanted in the home with a minimum of stress and maximum enjoyment. You have a great road map; you can follow it into your golden years or do it again, over and over, building a dream home every ten years or so to adjust to your changing home ownership needs.

As you've just discovered, building is a very detailed process. At Whitestone Custom Homes, we make it easy using our trademarked system. You can move forward using our nearly 30 years of experience building homes to your advantage. You will be one of the select few who really know how to achieve your home ownership goals in a personal, powerful and unique manner.

I've seen others who didn't take our advice. I have seen frustrations, disappointment, family squabbles, lost money, lost opportunity, even divorces and worse.

But, when you let experts do what they're paid to do, you can avoid that learn from the pros how to apply your personality to our expertise to create the custom home of your dreams. When you're ready, come visit us at http://whitestonehomes.com/ to see what we can do for you. We'll be glad to put you in the home of your dreams!

ABOUT THE AUTHOR

Tim Rice has spent nearly 30 years in the construction business, covering all aspects of planning, designing and building new custom homes. He is a Texas homebuilder with over two decades of experience, who founded Whitestone Custom Homes, Ltd. in San Antonio back in 1998. Tim saw a need there for a local builder that provided luxury custom design and quality at a competitive price. He founded his own company, Whitestone Custom Homes, which specializes in building new, upscale custom homes for creative, discerning, and satisfied clients!

Feel free to visit Whitestone Custom Homes online at (www.whitestonehomes.com), or contact Tim in the San Antonio headquarters, 3619 Paesano's Parkway. Suite 214, San Antonio, TX 78231.

Email: Tr@whitestonehomes.com

Office: 210-497-4334x205

Web: www.whitestonehomes.com

Facebook: www.facebook.com/#!/WhitestoneCustomHomes

Twitter: @WhiteStoneHomes

Blog: http://whitestonehomes.com/blog/

Made in the USA
Lexington, KY
22 March 2014